The Times Mirror Company is pleased to sponsor the Olympic Arts Festival, a joyous marriage of art and sport. The Festival has become what we hoped it would be: a major artistic statement, a clear reflection of the spirit of the Olympics, an arts festival for everyone.

The Olympic Arts Festival is multinational, multicultural and multilingual. Its artists come from the native lands of many Los Angeles citizens: from Mexico and South America, from Asia, Australia, Africa and Europe, and from elsewhere in Canada and the United States. The Festival occurs at a unique moment in the history of Los Angeles. It reflects the unprecedented cultural richness, diversity and quality that have been building for many years. Times Mirror, founded in Los Angeles 100 years ago, played a major role in that cultural development and in the growth of the city. For these reasons, we felt it was appropriate and important to give our support to the Olympics through the Arts Festival.

Times Mirror believes the arts belong to everyone. This belief is the cornerstone of our sponsorship of the Olympic Arts Festival. We know the arts provide a universal language that unites all of us and we believe that this Arts Festival embodies the spirit of the Olympic Games.

OTIS CHANDLER
Chairman of the Board & Editor-in-Chief

ROBERT F. ERBURU
President & Chief Executive Officer

DR. FRANKLIN D. MURPHY
Chairman of the Executive Committee

OLYMPIC
ARTS FESTIVAL

PUBLISHED BY
LOS ANGELES TIMES SYNDICATE

TEXT BY
ROBERT J. FITZPATRICK

ACKNOWLEDGEMENTS

EDITORIAL CONSULTANTS

Richard Frey

William Hackman

Nancy Berman Hathaway

Michael Kurcfeld

Dan Pavillard

Daniel Schillaci

OLYMPIC ARTS FESTIVAL STAFF

Robert J. Fitzpatrick, Director

Hope Tschopik, Associate Director

Peter Schneider, Associate Director

The 33 dedicated professional staff members and numerous volunteers deserve special recognition for the myriad, superior and essential contributions they made to the high quality and ultimate success of the 1984 Olympic Arts Festival.

CULTURAL AND FINE ARTS ADVISORY COMMISSION

Dorothy Chandler,
Honorary Chairwoman

Maureen Kindel, Chairwoman

Olive Behrendt, Camilla Frost,
Richard Sherwood, Vice Chairs

FESTIVAL CO-PRODUCERS

Academy of Motion Picture Arts and Sciences, Actors for Themselves, American Film Institute, ARCO Center for Visual Art, Brockman Gallery Productions, California/International Arts Foundation, California Institute of the Arts, California Museum of Afro-American History and Culture, The CAST Theatre, Center Theatre Group/Mark Taper Forum, City of Los Angeles, Craft and Folk Art Museum, The Dance Gallery, The Ensemble Studio Theatre of Los Angeles, Federated Philatelic Clubs of Southern California, Festival Music Incorporated, Frederick S. Wight Art Gallery, Bill Graham Presents, The Groundlings, Guber-Peters Company, The Huntington Library, Independent Composers Association, Japanese American Cultural and Community Center, KCET-TV, KUSC-FM, L.A. Theatre Works, Los Angeles Actors' Theatre, Los Angeles Area Dance Alliance, Los Angeles Center for Photographic Studies, Los Angeles County Museum of Art, Los Angeles County Museum of Natural History, Los Angeles International Film Exposition, Los Angeles Institute of Contemporary Art, Los Angeles Municipal Art Gallery, Los Angeles Philharmonic Association, Museum of Contemporary Art, Music Center Opera Association, Newport Harbor Art Museum, Odyssey Theatre, Pacific Asia Museum, Plaza de la Raza, The Port of Long Beach TOPSail '84 Committee, Room for Theatre, Santa Barbara Museum of Art, Social and Public Arts Resource Center, University Art Museum of UCSB, Pasadena Center & Pasadena Civic Auditorium/Theatre, Television Center, Studio 9, University of California, Los Angeles, The Victory Theatre

Produced for the Los Angeles Times Syndicate by Sequoia Communications
Design by Margo Chase   Printed in Japan
ISBN 0-917859-00-6

© Martine Franck, Magnum Photos, Inc.

TO THE ARTISTS, ATHLETES AND AUDIENCES

WHO PARTICIPATED IN THE OLYMPIC ARTS FESTIVAL

AND THE GAMES OF THE XXIIIRD OLYMPIAD

When Pierre de Coubertin established the Modern Games in 1896, he intended that they embody the spirit of the Ancient Games where intellectual virtuosity and artistic skill were celebrated as well as physical strength and prowess.

For the XXIIIrd Olympiad, the Los Angeles Olympic Organizing Committee chose to honor that tradition by creating a 10-week festival whose international character would reflect the Games and the host city of Los Angeles. The Committee gratefully acknowledges the generous and invaluable support of the Festival's official sponsor, The Times Mirror Company, in making the 1984 Olympic Arts Festival possible.

PAUL ZIFFREN
Chairman, LAOOC

PETER V. UEBERROTH
President, LAOOC

HARRY L. USHER
Executive Vice President
General Manager, LAOOC

John Baldessari, 1984 Olympic Fine Arts Poster Series

TABLE OF
CONTENTS

Sankaijuku

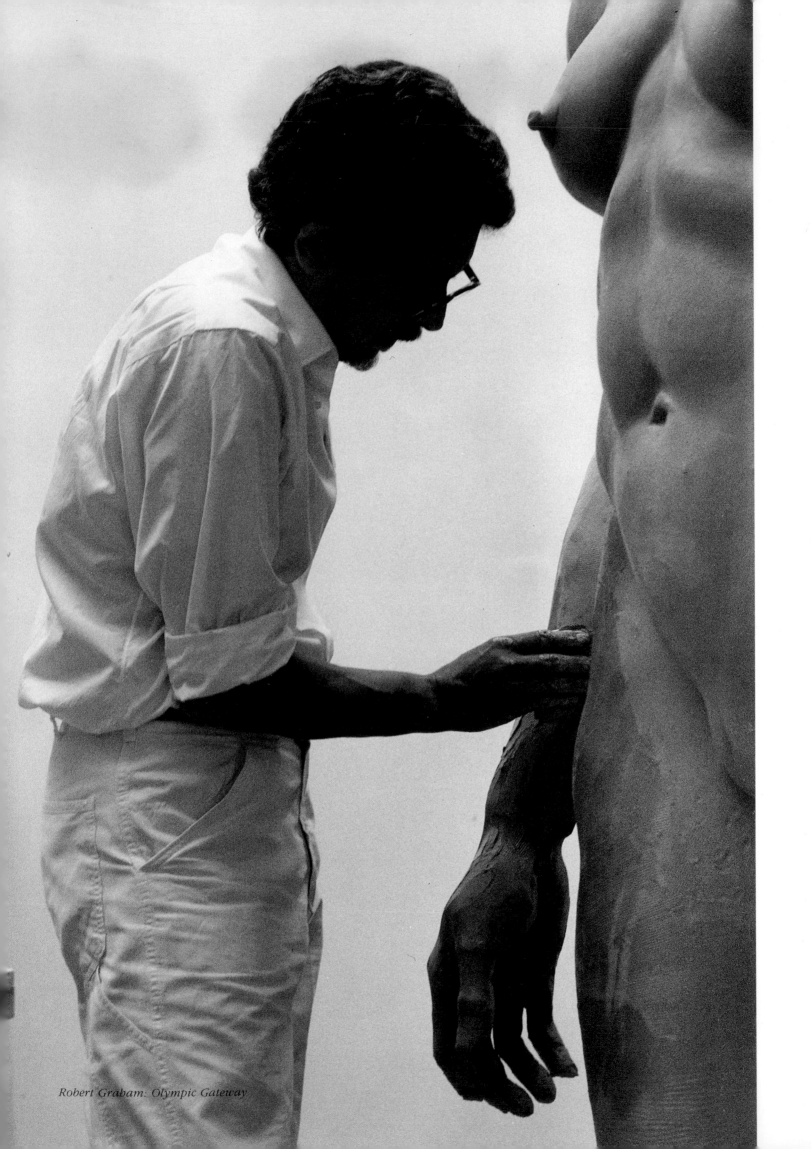

Robert Graham: Olympic Gateway

THE MAKING
OF THE FESTIVAL

———————

The making of the Olympic Arts Festival required four years, 300,000 miles of travel and the negotiation of more than 130 contracts with 18 countries. The project involved hammering out myriad details with artistic directors, company managers and curators, and negotiating with government officials ranging from ambassadors and ministers of culture and tourism to heads of state.

The Olympic Arts Festival began with the principle that art is not a form of propaganda but an instrument of truth, an opportunity to put aside differences and to rejoice in being alive. The guiding principle in selecting the exhibitions and performing arts companies that would participate in the Festival was that of excellence. Because it was the Olympics and because half the population of the human race would be looking at Los Angeles in the summer of 1984, the response was extraordinarily favorable.

Countries without diplomatic relations with one another, such as the People's Republic of China and the Republic of Korea, were content to appear on the same stage. Governments which might have preferred more traditional representatives of their cultures respected the artistic integrity of the Festival and provided substantial support for artists of untraditional bent. Thus, the Festival can offer the United States debuts of Pina Bausch's Wuppertaler Tanztheater, one of the most stimulating and unorthodox performing groups in the world today; and of Circus Oz, an Australian troupe that mixes rock music, political satire and high comedy with acrobatics, juggling and tight-rope walking.

Shipping three major operatic productions overseas, with elaborate sets, large casts and a full orchestra, is a formidable task. For this reason, The Royal Opera of Covent Garden has never before appeared in the United States. The occasion of the Olympics proved to be a sufficient stimulus to those who longed to bring the renowned company to this country; a consortium of backers was formed and logistical problems were resolved.

Similarly, precious art objects that otherwise might never have left home have been generously lent by museums and governments around the world. Forty-five of the Impressionist masterpieces on display at the Los Angeles County Museum of Art's *A Day in the Country: Impressionism and the French Landscape* represent an unprecedented loan from the Louvre. It is unlikely that such works shall ever travel en masse again once they are installed in Paris' new Musée d'Orsay. Persuading officials of the French Ministry of Culture to let these works fly halfway around the world might have been impossible were it not for an exhibition in the Olympic Arts Festival.

So, too, many of the ceremonial masks and robes and related artifacts that comprise *Bugaku: Treasures from the Kasuga Shrine* are centuries old and have never before been viewed outside the Shrine in Nara, Japan. So it was especially exciting for the Festival when the Shrine's chief priest inquired, "Would the people of Los Angeles be interested in sharing these with people from around the world during the Olympics?"

Not everything in the making of the Olympic Arts Festival was quite so easy, of course. Many of the same logistical problems faced in the mounting of the Games confronted the Festival's organizing staff as well: the care and feeding of 1,500 artists from around the world; the working out of contractual details in a multiplicity of languages; and the scheduling of some 400 events within the available limits of space and time.

Unlike those cities that host Europe's major arts festivals—Edinburgh with its castle, Avignon with its Palace of the Popes—Los Angeles has no great public monument which focuses attention and serves as a backdrop for the Festival. The city provides few opportunities for people to congregate: it is horizontal rather than vertical; vehicular and private rather than pedestrian and public. As such, Los Angeles might at first seem ill-suited to host an international arts festival.

One of the very first tasks facing the Festival's organizers, therefore, was rethinking the very idea of an arts festival. Here, again, there is a significant parallel with the organization of the 1984 Games. The decision was made to draw on what Los Angeles had to offer, rather than to bemoan what the city lacked. The Los Angeles Olympic Organizing Committee thus reached out to the city's vigorous arts community to enlist the support of its museums and galleries, its theatres and dance companies, its cultural and community centers. These organizations soon became co-producers of the Festival and have been instrumental in its planning and implementation.

There are other ways in which the Festival reflects the character of its host city. Los Angeles is strategically poised between two Easts: Europe/New York and the Orient. Tokyo, Seoul and Beijing are as influential here as Boston, Milan and Paris. Likewise, cultural traditions that date back to the days of the Spanish explorations of what are today California and Mexico combine with the city's openness to the new and untested to create an atmosphere unique in all the world. It is for this reason that the Festival deliberately set out to present performances and works that highlight these cultural traditions.

Whether one is speaking of The China Performing Arts Company, with its ensemble of musicians playing a variety of Chinese musical styles on traditional instruments, or the American Repertory Theatre staging Jonathan Miller's production of Sheridan's *The School for Scandal*, of the Korean National Dance Company or the Royal Winnipeg Ballet, the traditions of world culture are well represented. But the Festival is also distinctive in its presentation of works that bring these diverse traditions together and reveal the possibilities inherent in their interacting with one another.

One of the ways in which the Festival achieves such a blending of cultures is through the many "festivals-within-a-festival" taking place throughout the city. The Craft and Folk Art Museum's International Festival of Masks, like the Plaza de la Raza Folklife Festival, provides an opportunity for visitors from around the world to explore the traditions of cultures they might otherwise never have encountered.

The intermingling of cultures is perhaps most evident in the theatrical productions presented at the Festival. The Japanese company Waseda Sho-Gekijo offers an adaptation of *The Trojan Women* that reshapes this classic of Western drama into a tale told by an aging beggar-woman sifting through the rubble of post-war Tokyo. In a similar vein, L.A. Theatre Works, one of this city's distinguished theatres, has undertaken a production of *Agamemnon* as freely adapted by contemporary British playwright Steven Berkoff.

Three of the world's great acting companies—The Royal Shakespeare Company, Le Théâtre du

Soleil and Piccolo Teatro di Milano—bring Shakespeare alive in three different languages. Their productions draw on dramatic traditions as diverse as Japanese Kabuki, Indian Kathakali and the Italian baroque stage, as well as the more familiar Elizabethan tradition that was Shakespeare's own. In addition, The Goodman Theatre offers its neo-vaudevillean production of *The Comedy of Errors*, featuring the Flying Karamazov Brothers. This irreverent production recalls a too-often-forgotten aspect of theatre in general and of Shakespeare in particular—that it is a theatre not only of word, but of gesture, a theatre whose popular wellsprings are still evident.

But if such cultural cross-fertilization is most evident in theatre, it is no less the case for the other components of the Olympic Arts Festival. Modern choreographers Twyla Tharp, Alwin Nikolais and Eliot Feld have distinguished themselves for their willingness to incorporate disparate elements into their works, as have composers Rhys Chatam and John Cage, whose works are heard in the Contemporary Music Festival. And *Art in Clay* at the Municipal Gallery in Barnsdall Park features works by artists from around the world who have chosen to make California their home and who, together, put a distinctly regional imprint on the ceramic arts.

Another crucial focal point of the Festival is the presentation of works that mix media and challenge traditional artistic categories. Pina Bausch's dancers interrupt their choreographed movements to act out fantasies, speak to one another and even serve formal tea to the audience. Is it dance? Theatre?

And how would one categorize Morton Subotnick's *The Double Life of Amphibians?* Subotnick calls the piece a "staged tone-poem." Working with director Lee Breuer and designer Irving Petlin, Subotnick has fashioned a work that crosses a variety of artistic frontiers, including dance, theatre, music and design. Even within a single genre, such as music, Subotnick's three-part work, performed here in its entirety for the first time, moves freely from passages scored for voice and chamber ensemble to electronically generated sounds.

In like manner, Merce Cunningham's innovative mixing of media and collaborations with renowned artists and composers, notably John Cage, constitute a genre that is as much performance art as it is dance.

The Festival juxtaposes cultures, art forms, even whole epochs: In addition to the Bugaku dancers, masters of a form that dates back to the eighth century, Japan is represented by Sankaijuku, innovators in the dance form known as *butoh*, which heralds the 21st. *Automobile and Culture* at the Museum of Contemporary Art is an exhibition about that quintessentially modern icon, the car. Yet among the works displayed are visionary sketches and woodcuts by such Renaissance figures as Albrecht Dürer and Leonardo da Vinci. An Epidaurus Festival Production of *Oedipus Rex* telescopes the ancient and modern world, remaining faithful to the original text, yet demonstrating just how modern the work really is. And Mexico sends both the Ballet Folklorico de Guadalajara, one of the most carefully researched and, therefore, one of the most authentic of its folkloric companies, and the Teatro Taller Epico de la UNAM, a theatre ensemble inspired by the European avant-garde, yet performing a work based on an epic poem of Mexican history.

Finally, the Olympic Arts Festival juxtaposes emerging young talents with more established representatives of their fields. The California Dance Festival, for instance, provides a stage for many of California's finest young choreographers and dancers. And of the thirty participating theatre companies, several are relatively new and still carving out their identities. But nowhere is the delicate balance between the eagerly anticipated and the totally unexpected more evident than in the Chamber Music Festival, which offers the finest young chamber musicians in the world—winners of the most prestigious competitions in their fields—the opportunity to share the spotlight with such recognized masters as the Sequoia and Guarneri String Quartets. Such a pairing of the known and the unknown, the established and the emerging, is, after all, the essence of the Olympics.

In ancient Greece, the accomplishments of athletic heroes were recorded in sculpture, in poetry, and in paintings. Indeed, the regular gatherings at Olympia were celebrations not only of athletic prowess, but also of all that is excellent in humankind. The Greeks perceived a unity of form and content, of body and soul, that is often lost in the modern world. It was the hope of Pierre de Coubertin, the founder of the modern Olympics, to recapture that spirit of unity which was so apparent among the ancient Greeks. As early as 1906, Coubertin expressed his wish that the Olympics include not only sports competitions, but also celebrations of the arts; and it has been the goal of this Festival to return to the spirit of ancient Greece.

The names of most of the competitors in the ancient Games have been lost to the centuries. Their fastest times have not been recorded; but many of the scupltures do remain. They are an integral part of the legacy that ancient Greece has left to the modern world. Undoubtedly, the 1984 Olympic Arts Festival will leave a legacy of its own to the people of Los Angeles and Southern California.

It is difficult, if not impossible, to determine in advance what such a legacy might consist of. Some of the visible reminders might be obvious enough: the murals along the freeways between downtown and the Coliseum, the Fine Arts Poster Series, Robert Graham's monumental bronze Gateway facing the Coliseum in Exposition Park. But many of the most important elements may prove less tangible: a new spirit of cooperation and collaboration among the many outstanding arts organizations within the city; a new sense of what is possible within a community of artists that has already begun to test the outer limits of convention; a new understanding of the creative process for an audience that is not afraid of challenges.

The making of a festival is a process—a creative process. So, too, is the playing out of a festival a process. Perhaps there should be a verb that expresses the wonder and excitement of participating in a festival, that captures the spirit of individual, intensely personal exploration, discovery, recognition and, ultimately, re-creation. For the 1,500 artists, and for the audience of half a million, such a festival provides a mixture of exhilaration and exhaustion, tempting one to abandon normal patterns and to try all kinds of new experiences. If the Festival has worked for the audience, images will haunt the mind and remain on the retina long after the last performance and exhibition have ended.

Robert J. Fitzpatrick
Director, Olympic Arts Festival

Wuppertaler Tanztheater

THE
FESTIVAL

Circus Oz

Grupo de Teatro Macunaíma

The National Theatre of the Deaf

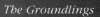
The Groundlings

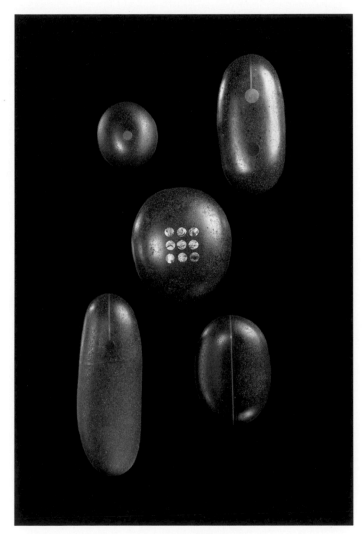

Kahurangi: Treasures from New Zealand

International Festival of Masks

The China Performing Arts Company

The Mosaic Image

Art in Clay

California Sculpture Show

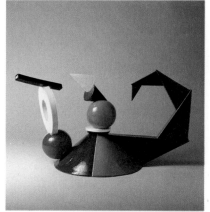

Art in Clay

Art in Clay

London Contemporary Dance Theatre

Olympiad of Animation

Theatre Sans Fil of Montreal, Quebec

San Francisco Ballet

Odyssey Theatre Ensemble

The Royal Shakespeare Company

Waseda Sho-Gekijo

Twyla Tharp Dance

Dance Theatre of Harlem

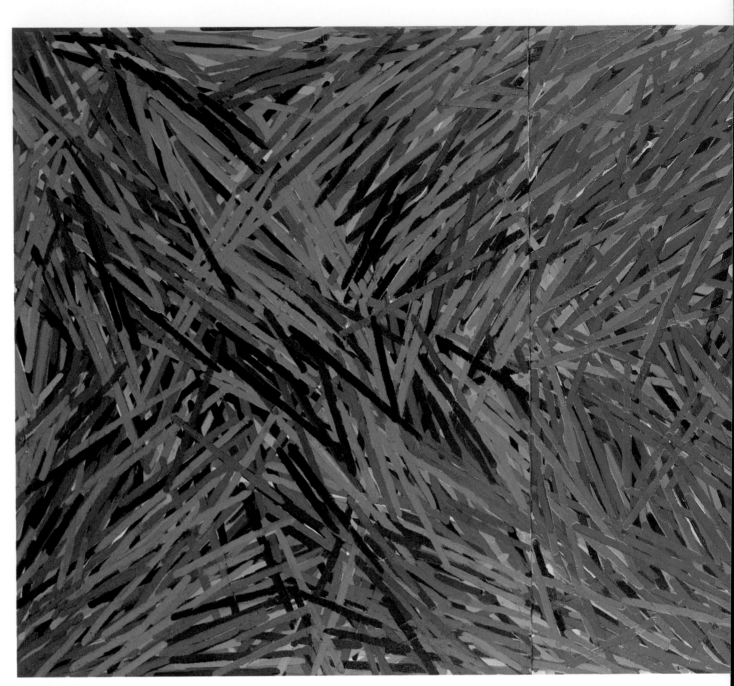

Art of the States

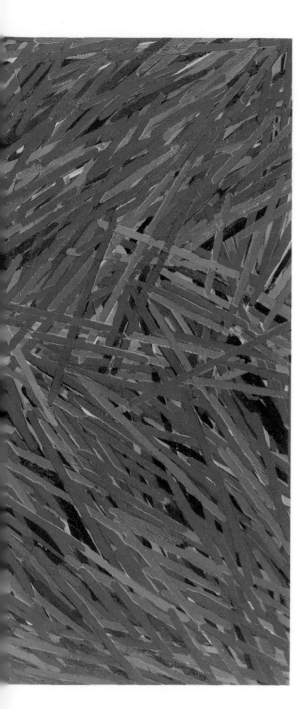

California Sculpture Show

51

The Feld Ballet

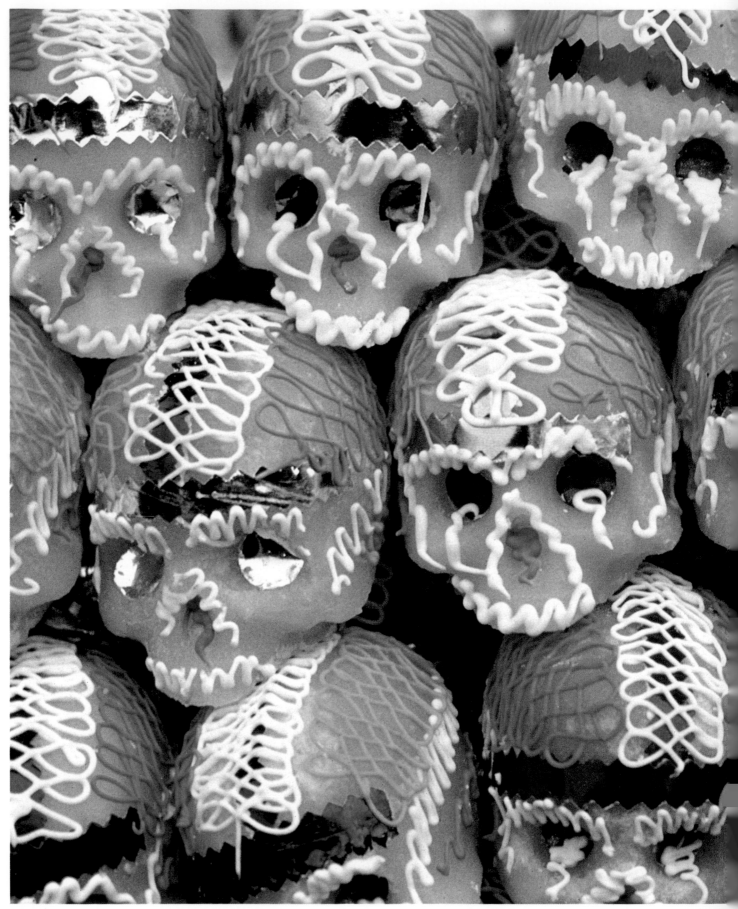

Plaza de la Raza

54

Masks in Motion

55

Carlos Almaraz: A Survey Exhibition

Australia: Nine Artists

Lewitzky Dance Company

Royal Winnipeg Ballet

Groupe Emile Dubois

A Day in the Country: Impressionism and the French Landscape

New Directions in New York/Bay Area Painting

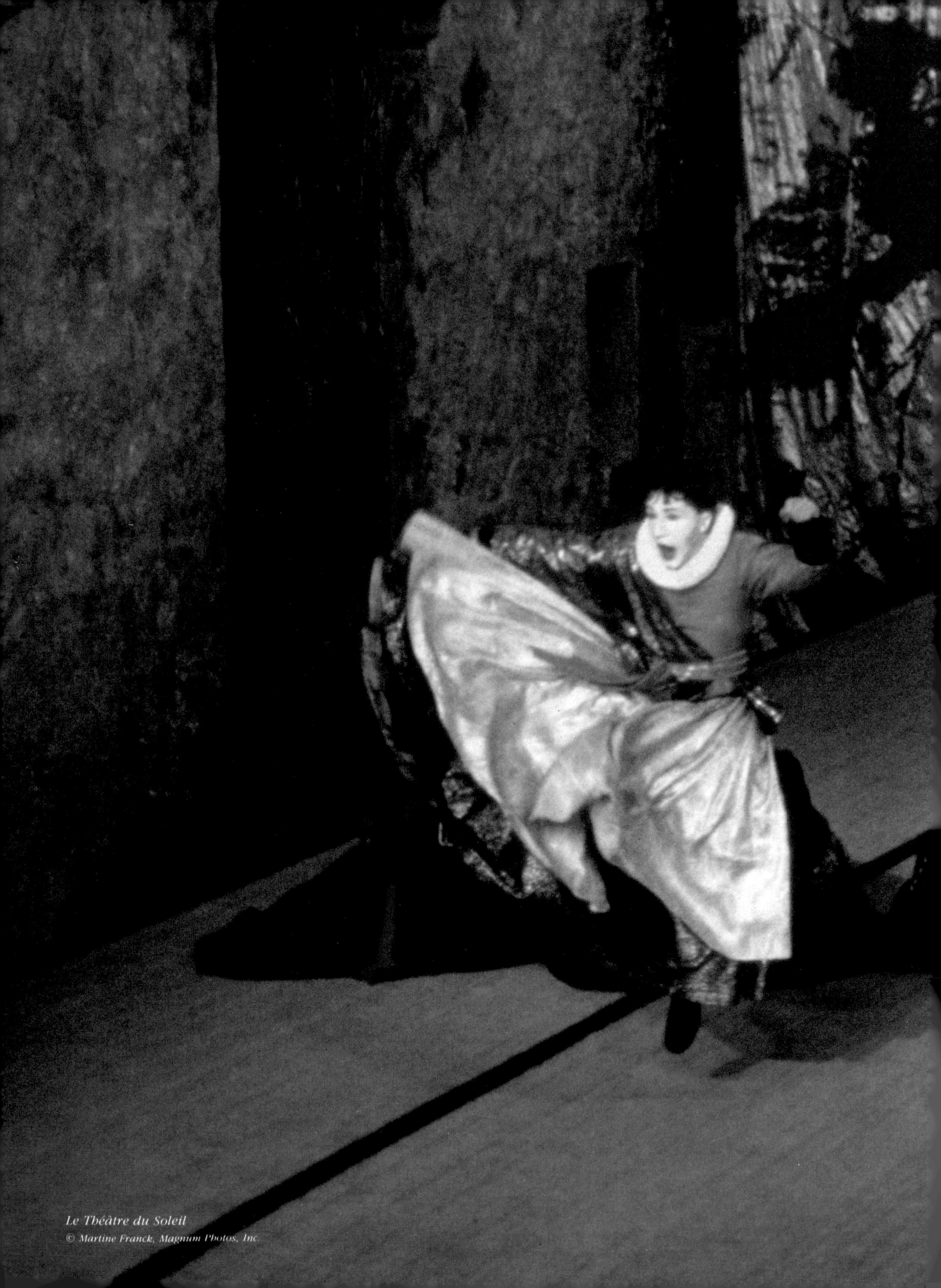

Le Théâtre du Soleil

Cricot 2

The Negro Ensemble Company

Guarneri String Quartet

Contemporary Music Festival

Sequoia String Quartet

Hagen String Quartet

Colorado String Quartet

Contemporary Music Festival

Les Ballets Africains

Kodo

The Royal Opera of Covent Garden

Los Angeles Actors' Theatre

Waseda Sho-Gekijo

The Royal Shakespeare Company

*Bugaku: Treasures
from the Kasuga Shrine*

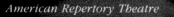

FESTIVAL ARTISTS

L. A. Theatre Works

Aman Folk Ensemble

The Victory Theatre

DANCE

Co-producer: The Dance Gallery
Artistic Director: Bella Lewitzky
Project Director: Darlene Neel

AMAN FOLK ENSEMBLE

Artistic Director: Don Sparks
Founding Artistic Director: Leona Wood
Associate Artistic Director: Mardi Rollow
Mexico: Fiesta Norteña (G. Armstrong);
Iran: Tadjikistan-Zang (G. Armstrong);
USSR: Uzbekistan-Samarkand (L. Wood);
Romania: Dances from Central Romania (B. Glass, R. Crum);
Yugoslavia: Lindjo (A. Shay, M. Taylor);
Tunisia: Wedding Dances (L. Wood);
Hungary-Transylvania: Hungarian Folk Dances (S. Timor);
Appalachia: Dances of the American South (B. Burke);
California Heritage Suite (R. Evanchuck)

BALLET FOLKLORICO DE GUADALAJARA

Artistic Director: Carlos Ernesto Ochoa
Authentic folk dances from the many regions of Mexico including Sonora, Vera Cruz, Jalisco and Chalapa

BUGAKU DANCE

Shinto Chief-Priest Kasuga-Taisha Shrine:
Rev. Chikatada Kazannoin
Project Director: Rev. Jou Kiyomi
Bugaku Dance

CALIFORNIA DANCE FESTIVAL

SF/LA Dance (San Francisco Bay Area Dance Coalition/Los Angeles Area Dance Alliance); Los Angeles Hispanic Dance Festival; Asian Pacific Dance Festival; 1984 Olympic Black Dance Festival; Kinetikos Choreographers Showcase

DANCE THEATRE OF HARLEM

Artistic Directors: Arthur Miller, Karel Shook
Four Temperaments; *Stars & Stripes*; *Serenade*; *Concerto Barocco*; *Agon* (G. Balanchine); *Fall River Legend* (A. de Mille); *Streetcar Named Desire* (V. Bettis); *Firebird* (J. Toras); *Le Corsaire* (K. Shook); *Troy Game* (R. North)

THE FELD BALLET

Artistic Director: Eliot Feld
Play Bach; *Straw Hearts*; and a third piece to be announced (E. Feld)

GROUPE EMILE DUBOIS

Artistic Director: Jean-Claude Gallotta
Ulysse (J. Gallotta)

KODO

Artistic Director: Toshio Kawauchi
Yamabushi-Kagura "Torimai"; *Hae*; *Miyake Daiko*; *Hachijo Daiko*; *Nishimonai Dance*; *Monochrome*; *Ayako-mai*; *O-daiko*; *Yatai-bayashi*

KOREAN NATIONAL DANCE COMPANY

Flower Crown Dance; *Love Song Dance*; *Fan Dance*; *Religious Exaltation*; *Kanggansullae*; *Story of Tomi* (B. Song); *Salp'uri*; *Farmers' Dance* (S. Ho Kook)

LEWITZKY DANCE COMPANY

Artistic Director: Bella Lewitzky
Confines; *Spaces Between*; *Inscape*; *Continuum*; and an untitled premiere (B. Lewitzky)

LES BALLETS AFRICAINS

Tam-Tam Concert; *Mooba*; *Soundiata Keita*; *The Sacred Forest*; *Finale*

LONDON CONTEMPORARY DANCE THEATRE

Artistic Directors: Robert Cohan, Siobhan Davies
Forest; *Class*; *Stabat Mater* (R. Cohan); *Run Like Thunder* (T. Jobe); *The Dancing Department*; and an untitled new work (S. Davies)

LOS ANGELES BALLET

Artistic Director: John Clifford
Swan Lake, Act II; *Capriccio* (G. Balanchine); *Copellia, Act III* (A. Danilova, from a piece by N. Sergeyev)

Merce Cunningham Dance Company

Los Angeles Ballet

The National Theatre of the Deaf

MERCE CUNNINGHAM
DANCE COMPANY

Artistic Director: Merce Cunningham
Trails; *Quartet*; *Locale*; *Coast Zone*;
Channels/Inserts; *Roadrunners*
(M. Cunningham)

NIKOLAIS DANCE THEATRE

Artistic Director: Alwin Nikolais
Liturgies; *Kaleidescope*; *Pond*; *Gallery*; and
an untitled new work (A. Nikolais)

ROYAL WINNIPEG BALLET

Artistic Director: Arnold Spohr
L'Estro Armonico (J. Cranko); *Lento, A
Tempo E Appasionata* (V. Nebrada); *Four
Last Songs* (R. van Dantzig); *Les Patineurs*
(F. Ashton); *Our Waltzes* (V. Nebrada);
Giselle pas de deux (L. Lavrosky); *Translu-
cent Tones* (N. Christe); *5 Tangos* (H. van
Mahen)

SAN FRANCISCO BALLET

Artistic Directors: Lew Christensen,
Michael Smuin
Selections from the company's repertoire,
including highlights from the 50th
Anniversary Gala

SANKAIJUKU

Artistić Director: Ushio Amagatsu
Jômôn Sho (U. Amagatsu)

TWYLA THARP DANCE

Artistic Director: Twyla Tharp
Telemann; *Lay Me Down*; *Nine Sinatra
Songs*; *Bad Smells* (T. Tharp)

PINA BAUSCH WUPPERTALER
TANZTHEATER

Artistic Director: Pina Bausch
Rite of Spring; *Cafe Müller*; *1980*;
Bluebeard (P. Bausch)

THEATRE

Co-producer: Center Theatre Group/
Mark Taper Forum
Artistic Director: Gordon Davidson
Project Director: Peter Schneider

ACTORS FOR THEMSELVES

Artistic Director: Joseph Stern
Untitled premiere

AMERICAN REPERTORY THEATRE

Artistic Director: Robert Brustein
The School for Scandal, Richard Sheridan
Director: Jonathan Miller
Six Characters in Search of an Author,
Luigi Pirandello
Directors: Andrei Serban, Robert Brustein

ANTENNA THEATRE

Artistic Director: Chris Hardman
Amnesia, Chris Hardman
Director: Chris Hardman

THE CAST THEATRE

Artistic Directors: Ted Schmitt, Randy
Clifton
Brain Hotel, The Director and Actors
Director: Tony Abatemarco

CENTER THEATRE GROUP/
MARK TAPER FORUM

Artistic Director: Gordon Davidson
The American Clock, Arthur Miller
Director: Gordon Davidson
Wild Oats, John O'Keefe, adapted by James
McClure
Director: Tom Moore

THE CHINA PERFORMING
ARTS COMPANY

Central Ensemble of National Music
Artistic Directors: Li Huanzi and Tang
Rongmei
Chengdu Acrobatic Troupe
Artistic Director: Wang Boying
Traditional music, dance and acrobatics

Room for Theatre

Actors for Themselves

Ballet Folklorico de Guadalajara

CIRCUS OZ

Artistic direction is collective.
Original production created by: Sue Broadway, Tim Coldwell, Kelvin Gedye, Jane Mullett, Alan Robertson, Geoff Toll, Ponch Hawkes, Georgine Sparks, Sallee Forth, Judy Pascoe, Jenny Saunders, Theresa Blake, Therese Cashew, Alan Clarke, Gael Coulton, Scott Grayland, Bruce Moshel

CARLO AND ALBERTO COLOMBAIONI

Original production: Carlo and Alberto Colombaioni

CRICOT 2

Artistic Director: Tadeusz Kantor
The Dead Class; *Wielopole-Wielopole*, Tadeusz Kantor
Director: Tadeusz Kantor

THE ENSEMBLE STUDIO THEATRE LOS ANGELES

Artistic Directors: Thomas Callaway, Sara Cunningham, Carla Meyer, Jenny O'Hara
Sporting Goods, Members of the Ensemble Studio Theatre
Director: Members of the Ensemble Studio Theatre

THE GOODMAN THEATRE/ FLYING KARAMAZOV BROTHERS

Artistic Director: Gregory Mosher
The Comedy of Errors, William Shakespeare
Director: Robert Woodruff

THE GROUNDLINGS

Artistic Director: Tom Maxwell
Olympic Trials, A Chick Hazard Mystery, Phil Hartman, Tom Maxwell and company
Director: Tom Maxwell

GRUPO DE TEATRO MACUNAÍMA

Artistic Director: Antunes Filho
Macunaíma, adapted by Jacques Thierot e Grupo de Arte Paul Brazil, from the novel by Mario de Andrade
Director: Antunes Filho

LOS ANGELES ACTORS' THEATRE

Producing Artistic Director: Bill Bushnell
Sherlock's Last Case, Charles Marowitz
Director: Robert Benedetti

L.A. THEATRE WORKS

Producing Director: Susan Albert Loewenberg
Agamemnon, Aeschylus
Director: Steven Berkoff

DE MEXICAANSE HOND

Artistic Director: Alex van Warmerdam
The Class, Lookin's for a Face, There's an Indian Around, Alex van Warmerdam
Director: Alex van Warmerdam

THE NATIONAL THEATRE OF THE DEAF

Artistic Director: David Hays
The Hero with a Thousand Faces, adapted from the book by Joseph Campbell
Director: Larry Arrick

AN EPIDAURUS FESTIVAL PRODUCTION

Oedipus Rex, Sophocles
Director: Minos Volanakis

THE NEGRO ENSEMBLE COMPANY

Artistic Director: Douglas Turner Ward
A Soldier's Play, Charles Fuller
Director: Douglas Turner Ward

NIGHTFIRE

Artistic Director: Laura Farabough
Liquid Distance/Timed Approach, Laura Farabough
Director: Laura Farabough

ODYSSEY THEATRE ENSEMBLE

Artistic Director: Ron Sossi
Edmond, David Mamet
Director: Ron Sossi

PICCOLO TEATRO DI MILANO

Artistic Director: Giorgio Strehler
Harlequin, The Servant of Two Masters, Carlo Goldoni
Director: Ferruccio Soleri
The Tempest, William Shakespeare
Director: Giorgio Strehler
Translator: Agostino Lombardo

RADEIS INTERNATIONAL

Artistic direction is collective.
Scaffoldings, Jos de Pauw, Pat van Hemlrijk, Dirk Pauwels, Georges Broeckaert

88

Carlo and Alberto Colombaioni

De Mexicaanse Hond

The CAST

ROOM FOR THEATRE

Artistic Directors: Delores Mann, Beverly Sanders, Sylvia Walden
Skylark, Samson Raphaelson
Director: Norman Cohen

THE ROYAL SHAKESPEARE COMPANY

Artistic Directors: Trevor Nunn, Terry Hands
Cyrano de Bergerac, Edmond Rostand
Translator: Anthony Burgess
Much Ado About Nothing, William Shakespeare
Director: Terry Hands

TEATRO TALLER EPICO DE LA UNAM

Artistic Director: Luis de Tavira
Novedad de la Patria, Luis de Tavira, based on a poem by Lopez Velard
Director: Luis de Tavira

THÉÂTRE SANS FIL OF MONTREAL, QUÈBEC

Artistic Directors: Andre Viens, Claire Ranger
The Hobbit, J.R.R. Tolkien
Director: Claire Ranger

LE THÉÂTRE DU SOLEIL

Artistic Director: Ariane Mnouchkine
Henry IV, Part I; Richard II; Twelfth Night,
William Shakespeare
Director: Ariane Mnouchkine
Translator: Ariane Mnouchkine

THE VICTORY THEATRE

Artistic Directors: Tom Ormeny, Maria Gobetti
Back to Back, Al Brown
Director: Tom Ormeny

WASEDA SHO-GEKIJO

Artistic Director: Tadashi Suzuki
The Trojan Women, Euripides
Director: Tadashi Suzuki

MUSIC AND OPERA

CHAMBER MUSIC FESTIVAL

Co-producer: KUSC-FM
General Manager: Wallace A. Smith
Project Director: MaryAnn Bonino

Colorado String Quartet: Julie Rosenfeld, violin; Deborah Redding, violin; Francesca Martin, viola; Sharon Prater, cello
Program: Haydn, *Quartet in G Major, Opus 33, No. 5*; Laderman, *String Quartet No. 7 (1983)*; Beethoven, *Quartet in E Minor, Opus 59, No. 2*

Guarneri String Quartet: Arnold Steinhardt, violin; John Dalley, violin; Michael Tree, viola; David Soyer, cello
Program: Beethoven, *Quartet in A Major, Opus 18, No. 5*; Beethoven, *Grosse Fuga in B-Flat Major, Opus 133*; Beethoven, *Quartet in A Minor, Opus 132*

Hagen String Quartet: Lukas Hagen, violin; Annette Bik, violin; Veronika Hagen, viola; Clemens Hagen, cello
Program: Mozart, *Quartet in D Major, K. 575*; Kodály, *Quartet in D Major, Opus 10, No. 2*; Schubert, *Quartet in A Minor, D. 804*

Sequoia String Quartet: Yoko Matsuda, violin; Miwako Watanabe, violin; James Dunham, piano; Robert Martin, cello
Program: Mozart, *Quartet in C Major, K. 465, "Dissonant"*; Bartók, *Quartet No. 2, Opus 17*; Mendelssohn, *Octet in E-Flat Major for Strings, Opus 20* (with the Colorado String Quartet).

Winners of the Naumburg and Coleman Chamber Music Awards: To be announced

Winners of the 32nd Munich International Music Competition: Peter Matzka, violin; Teresa Turner-Jones, piano
Program: Brahms, *Violin Sonata in G Major, Opus 78*; Ives, *Sonata No. 2*; Schubert, *Fantasy in C Major, D. 934*

CLASSIC POPS AT THE BOWL

Co-producer: Los Angeles Philharmonic Association
Executive Director: Ernest Fleischmann
Project Director: Robert Harth
Los Angeles Philharmonic, Executive Director: Ernest Fleischmann
Los Angeles Master Chorale, Music Director: Roger Wagner
Program: Music by Rogers, Hart & Hammerstein
Conductor: John Green

Antenna Theatre

Goodman Theatre/Flying Karamazov Brothers

The Ensemble Studio Theatre Los Angeles

CONTEMPORARY MUSIC FESTIVAL

Co-producer: California Institute of the Arts
President: Robert J. Fitzpatrick
Project Director: Franz van Rossum
Program: Karlheinz Stockhausen, *Sternklang*; Morton Subotnick, *The Double Life of Amphibians*; Charles Dodge, *The Waves*; Roger Reynolds, *Transfigured Winds*; Sal Martirano, *Thrown*; Rhys Chatham, a new work for eleven instruments; John Cage, *Variations IV, improvisations*; CCMC/Toronto; IRCAM—John Chorning, York Hollèr, Gilbert Amy, Tod Machover, et al, with performances by members of the Los Angeles Philharmonic

THE GREAT OLYMPIC JAZZ MARATHON

Co-producer: Los Angeles Philharmonic Association
Executive Director: Ernest Fleischmann
Project Director: Robert Harth
Count Basie and Orchestra, The Crusaders, Free Flight, Bob James, Wynton Marsalis, Joe Williams

OLYMPIC JAZZ FESTIVAL

Co-producer: Festival Music Incorporated
Artistic Director: Tommy Vig
Arranger-conductor: Tommy Vig
Ernie Watts, Shelley Manne, Benny Carter, Jack Sheldon, Abraham Laboriel, Louie Bellson, Charlie Haden and others

PRELUDE TO THE OLYMPICS: A GALA CONCERT

Co-producer: Los Angeles Philharmonic Association
Executive Director: Ernest Fleischmann
Project Director: Robert Harth
Los Angeles Philharmonic, Executive Director: Ernest Fleischmann
Los Angeles Master Chorale, Music Director: Roger Wagner
Program: John Williams, *Olympic Fanfare*; Leonard Bernstein, *Prelude, Fugue, Chorale & Riffs*; Morton Gould, *American Song Cycle*; Aaron Copland, *Fanfare and Fugue, Symphony No. 3*; Beethoven, *Symphony No. 9 (Choral), Finale*
Conductor: Michael Tilson Thomas

THE ROYAL OPERA OF COVENT GARDEN

Co-producer: The Music Center Opera Association
President, Chief Executive Officer: Thomas Wachtell
Program Directors: Suzanne Sty, Rebecca Rickman
Music Director & Conductor: Sir Colin Davis
Program: Mozart, *Die Zauberflöte*, produced by August Everding; Puccini, *Turandot*, produced by Andrei Serban; Britten, *Peter Grimes*, produced by Elijah Moshinsky

SOUNDS IN MOTION

Co-producer: Independent Composers Association
President: Harry Gilbert
Project Director: Carl Stone
To be broadcast on KUSC-FM.
Compositions by: Charles Amirkhanian, John Cage, Paul Dresher, Joan La Barbara, Pauline Oliveros, Carl Stone

THE WESTMINSTER ABBEY MESSIAH

Co-producer: Los Angeles Philharmonic Association
Executive Director: Ernest Fleischmann
Project Director: Robert Harth
Program: Handel, *Messiah*
Conductor: Christopher Hogwood

OLYMPIAD OF POPULAR MUSIC

Co-producer: Bill Graham Presents
Executive Director: Bill Graham
Various artists to be announced

VISUAL ARTS

A DAY IN THE COUNTRY: IMPRESSIONISM AND THE FRENCH LANDSCAPE

Co-producer: Los Angeles County Museum of Art
Director: Dr. Earl A. Powell III
Curators: Dr. Earl A. Powell III, Scott Schaefer, Rich Bretell

Radeis International

Teatro Taller Epico de la UNAM

Nightfire

Organized by: Los Angeles County Museum of Art in collaboration with The Art Institute of Chicago, Réunion des Musées Nationaux de Paris
Location: Los Angeles County Museum of Art

CARLOS ALMARAZ:
A SURVEY EXHIBITION

Co-producer: Los Angeles Municipal Art Gallery, Barnsdall Park
Director & Curator: Josine Ianco-Starrels
Location: Los Angeles Municipal Art Gallery, Barnsdall Park

ART IN CLAY 1950s-1980s
IN SOUTHERN CALIFORNIA

Co-producer: Los Angeles Municipal Art Gallery, Barnsdall Park
Director: Josine Ianco-Starrels
Curator: Betty Sheinbaum
Location: Los Angeles Municipal Art Gallery, Barnsdall Park

ART OF THE STATES: AMERICAN
WORKS AFTER THE 60s

Co-producer: Santa Barbara Museum of Art
Director: Richard V. West
Curator: Robert McDonald
Location: Santa Barbara Museum of Art

AUSTRALIA: NINE
CONTEMPORARY ARTISTS

Co-producer: Los Angeles Institute of Contemporary Art
Director & Curator: Robert Smith
Artists: John Davis and Marr Grounds, Lyndal Jones and John Dunkley-Smith, Mike Parr and Stelarc, John Nixon and Redback Graphics
Location: Los Angeles Institute of Contemporary Art

THE AUTOMOBILE AND CULTURE

Co-producer: The Temporary Contemporary, Museum of Contemporary Art
Director: Richard Koshalek
Curator: Pontus Hulton
Location: The Temporary Contemporary, Museum of Contemporary Art

THE BLACK OLYMPIANS: 1904–1984

Co-producer: California Museum of Afro-American History & Culture
Director: Aurelia Brooks
Curator: Lonnie Bunch
Location: California Museum of Afro-American History & Culture

BUGAKU: TREASURES FROM
THE KASUGA SHRINE

Co-producer: Japanese American Cultural and Community Center
Director: Gerald D. Yoshitomi
Curator: Morihiro Ogawa, Miles Kubo
Organized by: Japanese American Cultural and Community Center, Boston Museum of Fine Arts, and Kasuga Shrine Foundation
Location: George J. Doizaki Gallery, Japanese American Cultural and Community Center

CALIFORNIA SCULPTURE SHOW

Co-producer: California International Arts Foundation
Director: Lyn Kienholz
Sculptors: Robert Arneson, Charles Arnoldi, Bruce Beasley, Fletcher Benton, Guy Dill, Jud Fine, Tom Holland, Robert Hudson, Manuel Neri, Sam Richardson, Michael Todd, DeWain Valentine
Curator: Henry Hopkins
Location: Fisher Gallery, University of Southern California

IN CONTEXT

Co-producer: The Temporary Contemporary, Museum of Contemporary Art
Director: Richard Koshalek
Artists: Douglas Heubler, Michael Heizer, Mobile Image, Betye Saar
Curator: Julia Brown
Location: The Temporary Contemporary, Museum of Contemporary Art

KAHURANGI: TREASURES
FROM NEW ZEALAND

Co-producer: Pacific Asia Museum
Director & Curator: David Kamanski
Location: Pacific Asia Museum

LOS ANGELES AND THE PALM TREE:
IMAGE OF A CITY

Co-producer: ARCO Center for Visual Art
Curator & Director: Fritz Frauchiger
Location: ARCO Center for Visual Art

L.A. and the Palm Tree

Olympic Philatelic Exhibition

LOS ANGELES... LEGACIES OF THE 1932 OLYMPICS

Co-producers: The City of Los Angeles
Organizer: Craig Lawson, Office of Mayor Tom Bradley
Location: Los Angeles City Hall, Los Angeles Central Library

MASKS IN MOTION

Co-producer: Craft and Folk Art Museum
Directors: Patrick H. Ela, Edith R. Wyle
Curator: Edith R. Wyle
Location: Craft and Folk Art Museum

THE MOSAIC IMAGE: THE FIRST TWENTY YEARS OF THE MUSEUM OF CULTURAL HISTORY

Co-producer: Museum of Cultural History, University of California, Los Angeles
Director: Dr. Christopher Donnan
Curator: Barbara A. Birney
Location: Frederick S. Wight Art Gallery, University of California, Los Angeles

OLYMPIC GATEWAY

Architect & Sculptor: Robert Graham
Location: Los Angeles Memorial Coliseum

OLYMPIC PHILATELIC EXHIBITION (OLYMPHILEX)

Co-producer: Federated Philatelic Clubs of Southern California
Director: Robert de Violini
Location: Pasadena Center Conference Building

OLYMPIC ROWING: INTEGRITY AND TRADITION

Co-producer: University Art Museum, University of California, Santa Barbara
Director & Curator: David Farmer
Location: University Art Museum, University of California, Santa Barbara

RETROSPECTIVE OF THE 1932 OLYMPIC GAMES

Co-producer: Los Angeles County Museum of Natural History
Director: Dr. Craig Black
"USA 1932"
Curator: Burt Reiner
"The 1932 Automobile Salon"
Curator: James Zordich
"The Games of the Xth Olympiad"
Curator: John Cahoon
Location: Los Angeles County Museum of Natural History

STUDIES FOR THE OLYMPIC GATEWAY

Co-producer: ARCO Center for Visual Art
Artist: Robert Graham
Director & Curator: Fritz Frauchiger
Location: ARCO Center for Visual Art

NEW DIRECTIONS IN NEW YORK/ BAY AREA PAINTING

Co-producer: Newport Harbor Art Museum
Director: Kevin Consey
"Action/Precision: The New Direction in New York 1955–1960"
Artists: Norman Bluhm, Michael Goldberg, Grace Hartigan, Al Held, Alfred Leslie, Joan Mitchell
Curator: Paul Schimmel
"The Figurative Mode: Bay Area Painting 1955–1965"
Artists: Elmer Bischoff, Richard Diebenkorn, David Park, Paul Wonner
Curator: Christopher Knight
Organizer: The Grey Art Gallery, New York University
Location: Newport Harbor Art Museum

FILM AND FESTIVALS

FILMEX '84

Co-producer: Los Angeles International Film Exposition
Executive Director: Suzanne McCormick
Artistic Director: Ken Wlaschin

THE GREAT WALL OF LOS ANGELES

Co-producer: Social and Public Arts Resource Center
Director: Judy Baca
Location: Tujunga Wash Control Channel

Hollywood Bowl

Los Angeles International Film Exposition

Olympiad of Animation

INTERNATIONAL FESTIVAL OF MASKS

Co-producer: Craft and Folk Art Museum
Directors: Patrick H. Ela and Edith R. Wyle
Producing Director: Willow Young
Location: Pan Pacific Park

A JAPANESE FESTIVAL

Co-producer: The Huntington Library Art Gallery & Botanical Gardens
Director & Organizer: Robert Middlekauff
Location: The Huntington Library Art Gallery & Botanical Gardens

1984 NATIONAL VIDEO FESTIVAL OLYMPICS SCREENING

Co-producer: The American Film Institute
Director: James Hindman
Associate Director: Jacqueline Kain
Location: The American Film Institute Campus

OLYMPIC MURAL PROJECT

Co-producer: Brockman Gallery Productions
Director: Alonzo Davis
Artists: Judy Baca, Glenna Boltuch, Alonzo Davis, Willie Heron, Frank Romero, Terry Schoonhoven, Roderick Sykes, Kent Twitchell, John Wehrle, Richard Wyatt

1984 OLYMPIC PHOTOGRAPHIC COMMISSION

Co-producer: Los Angeles Center for Photographic Studies
Photographers: Louis Bernal, JoAnn Callis, Jack Carnell, Robert Cumming, Jim Dow, Peter Reiss, Joel Sternfeld, Charles Traub, Bonnie Donahue, Frank Stewart
Director: Howard Spector
Location: The Temporary Contemporary, Museum of Contemporary Art
Director: Richard Koshalek

THE OLYMPIC FINE ARTS POSTER SERIES

Publisher: Knapp Communications
Chairman: Cleon Knapp
Project Manager: T. Swift Lockard
Artists: Carlos Almaraz, John Baldessari, Jennifer Bartlett, Lynda Benglis, Billy Al Bengston, Jonathan Borofsky, Richard Diebenkorn, April Greiman & Jayme Odgers, Sam Francis, David Hockney, Roy Lichtenstein, Martin Puryear, Robert Rauschenberg, Raymond Saunders, Gary Winogrand

THE OLYMPIAD OF ANIMATION

Co-producer: Academy of Motion Picture Arts & Sciences in association with International Animated Film Association (ASIFA)
Program Coordinator: Doug Edwards
Organizer: Prescott Wright
Location: Academy of Motion Picture Arts & Sciences, Samuel Goldwyn Theatre

PLAZA DE LA RAZA FOLKLIFE FESTIVAL

Co-producer: Plaza de la Raza, Lincoln Park
Director: Edmundo Rodriguez
Project Director: Dr. Miguel Dominguez
Location: Plaza de la Raza, Lincoln Park

TOPSAIL '84

Co-producer: The Port of Long Beach
Organizer: Elmar Baxter
Location: Marina Del Rey to Huntington Beach to Long Beach

  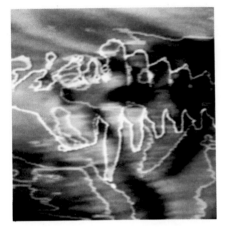

1984 Video Festival Olympics Screening

LIST OF ILLUSTRATIONS

Olympic Mural Project

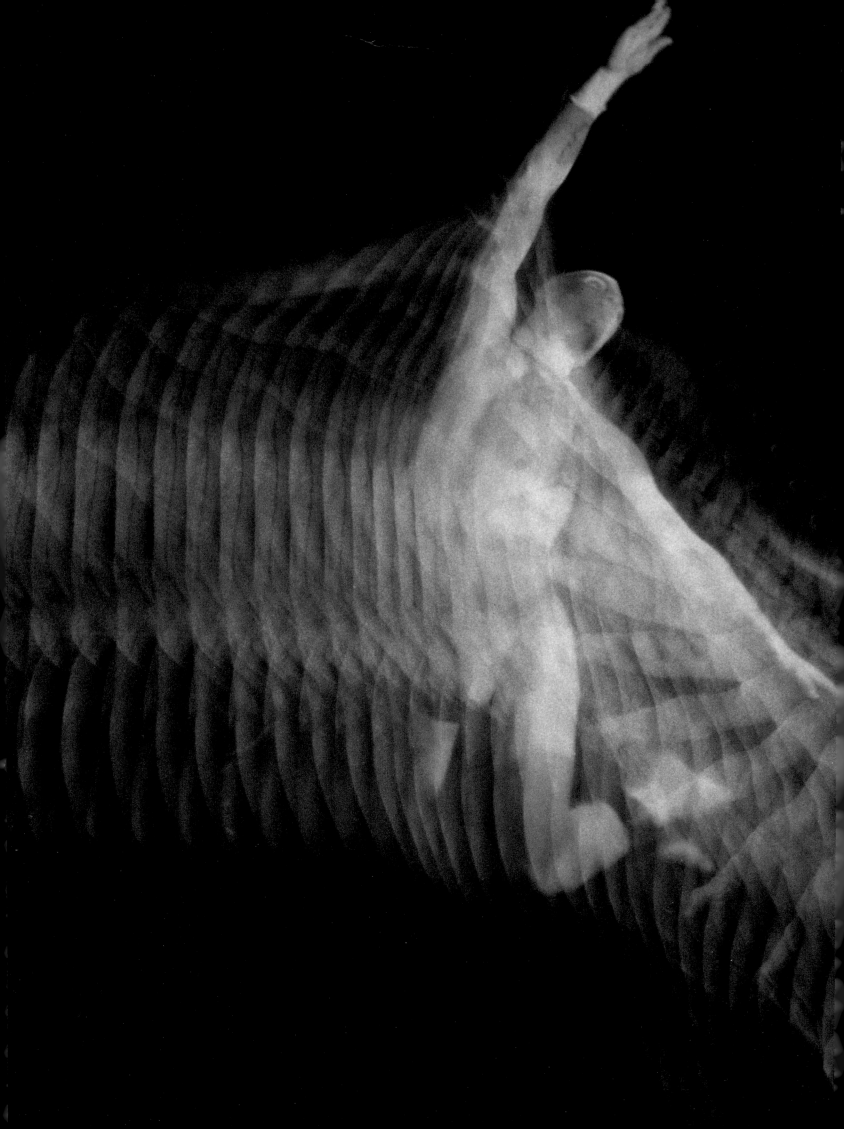